DATE DUE		
OCT 10 95			
JUL 2 2 00			
FE 03 '01			
JY 19 '02			
MAY 2 7 2003			

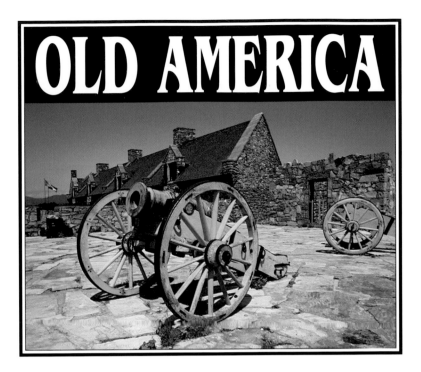

OLD AMERICA

Forts

Lynn Stone

Rourke Publications, Inc.
Vero Beach, FL 32964

Edited by Sandra A. Robinson

PHOTO CREDITS
All photos © James P. Rowan except p. 10 © Lynn M. Stone.

Library of Congress Cataloging-in-Publication Data

Stone, Lynn M.
    Forts / by Lynn Stone.
    p. cm. — (Old America)
    Summary: Discusses different types of forts and their uses and surveys the forts of North America.
    ISBN 0-86625-447-1
    1. Fortification – United States – Juvenile literature.
2. United States – History, Military – Juvenile literature.
[1. Fortification.] I. Title II. Series: Stone, Lynn M. Old America.
E159.S77 1993
355.7'0973—dc20   93-142
                                                                 CIP
                                                                 AC

Printed in the USA

TABLE OF CONTENTS

FORTS

Union gunfire began to blast away brick walls, forcing Fort Pulaski's surrender.

Shells from big **artillery** guns shrieked overhead and exploded into the fort. The fort's guns returned the fire, sending deadly missiles toward the Union Army's positions. The thunder of battle was deafening. Fort Pulaski, the brick fort that was "as strong as the Rocky Mountains," had been built to survive any attack. Still, Colonel Charles Olmstead, who commanded this Confederate fort, realized that he and the fort's 385 defenders had a frightening problem. Shells from the Union cannons had smashed through one of the $7\frac{1}{2}$-foot thick walls. Colonel Olmstead knew that soon the hail of Union gunfire would rip into the fort's northwest **magazine**. The magazine stored the fort's gunpowder. If struck by gunfire, the magazine would explode. The blast would destroy not only the magazine, but most of the fort's defenders as well.

The battle for Fort Pulaski occurred in Savannah, Georgia, in April, 1862. This was during the American Civil War (1861-65), the war fought between the states of the North and the South. The punishing duel of big guns lasted just 30 hours. Confederate Colonel Olmstead made the only sensible decision: he surrendered the fort. After the surrender of Fort Pulaski, the role of forts in North America was never the same. Oh, there was other fighting at forts in the South during the Civil War, notably at Fort Donelson, Tennessee. However, the Northern army's big guns had proven that even a **masonry** fort, one built of stone or brick, could be destroyed by gunfire. The fall of Fort Pulaski signalled

Fort Pulaski's Confederate guns returned fire, but were silenced after 30 hours of battle.

the beginning of the end for masonry forts. The fire-power of cannons and other big guns had become too mighty for fort walls. The ability of forts to defend their men and cities was rapidly disappearing. Warfare was changing. Forts were soon to be like dinosaurs — just historical curiosities.

From the mid-1500s through the 1870s, forts were important in North America. Forts were built for many purposes, and in many shapes and sizes. Generally, a fort was a group of buildings in an open area enclosed by an outer wall. The wall offered protection for the buildings and people within it. Fort defenders could fire rifles and heavy cannons at their enemies through openings in the outer wall.

Forts were built in **strategic** locations, places where they would be most useful. Some forts protected coastal towns from attack by ships. Fort Pulaski, for example, was built on an island where it could fire at enemy ships that might dare to sail up the Savannah River to Savannah.

Men dressed in authentic 18th century British uniforms relive the duties of the garrison at Fort Niagra in New York.

A fort's usefulness often went beyond defending a city, or guarding a trail or waterway. Forts provided armies with bases from which they could operate. Forts were built in wilderness areas so that soldiers could fight, explore, enforce laws and defend settlers. Later, the fort's soldiers, called its **garrison**, could return to the fort for safety, rest and supplies. The wilderness fort was a crude home for soldiers, away from the bustle of cities. The wilderness fort also offered a safe home for settlers when warfare broke out. People from the outlying areas often visited the forts to camp and trade. Trappers, settlers, Native Americans and merchants gathered to exchange furs and other goods, such as clothing, beads, knives, guns, ammunition and kettles.

Fort Union was a trading post in North Dakota. It brought settlers, traders and Native Americans together to swap goods.

Fort Union in North Dakota was built strictly as a trading post. Another trading post was Fort William, built by the Northwest Company of Canada in 1816. Fort William was the scene of the yearly Great Rendezvous, a loud, happy gathering of Native Americans, trappers and traders in Thunder Bay, Ontario.

One of the first forts built in North America was Fort Caroline. In 1564 a group of French **colonists**, or settlers, built the fort of wood and earth near present-day Jacksonville, Florida. Later, hundreds of forts were built in North America by the French, Spanish, British and Americans. Most of the original forts no longer exist. Weather, warfare and fire destroyed some. Others were torn apart for building materials, or because a growing

Fort Bowie's remains stand crumbling in the Arizona desert where U.S. Army soldiers were sent to fight Apaches.

Historic Fort Wayne in Indiana is now a part of the big city that borrowed its name.

town needed the fort's land. Some towns, of course, bear the names of the forts that actually started the towns. Have you heard of Fort Wayne, Indiana, or Fort Lauderdale, Florida? Many original forts remain in **restored**, or repaired, condition, like the Castillo de San Marcos in Florida and Fort Pulaski. Other forts — Clatsop, Erie, George, Meigs, Stanwix and Ticonderoga among them — have been accurately rebuilt to look like they did before they were destroyed long ago.

III TYPES OF FORTS

Palisades guard the rebuilt Fort Stanwix in New York.

The location of a fort and its purpose determined its construction materials. Coastal forts were built largely of earth, stone, logs, brick or combinations of those materials. They needed to be strong enough to survive shelling by cannons and other big guns from land and sea. Some forts built of stone or brick were shielded by mounds of earth. Others had sharpened wooden stakes, called **palisades**, as a fence.

Until about 1835, most warfare in North America had been in the eastern states and eastern Canada. Few settlers had moved west of the Great Lakes or the Appalachian Mountains. Battles and land buyouts changed that situation. The United States took ownership of huge chunks of land in the West during the early 1800s and bought Florida from Spain. As settlers began to stream westward into the new territories, a network of forts grew in the West. Unlike the great stone forts of the East, Western forts were usually built of logs. Fort defenders did not have to worry about being attacked by cannon fire. Western forts were built to establish law in wild country and to protect the growing rush of westbound pioneers from Native American attack. Native Americans saw the pioneers as a threat to their way of life. As Native American attacks grew in number, the American Army responded with more soldiers and forts. By the 1880s, the Native American wars were over. Tribes were forced onto government lands called **reservations**. The West was no longer a wild, untamed frontier. Railroads reached from New York to

In a living history exhibit at Fort Osage in Missouri, a woman makes natural dye in a kettle.

Fort Edgecomb, a blockhouse fort in Maine, was armed in the early 1800s for defense against a British invasion.

California. Frontier forts were no longer necessary. Forts Laramie, Larned, Bowie, and the rest, were left to decay.

The word "fort" almost always brings to mind strong walls around army buildings. Many so-called forts, such as Fort Edgecomb in Maine, were simply **blockhouses**. They were wooden buildings, usually two stories tall. They were not always surrounded by outer walls. Their defense sometimes depended entirely upon the sharpshooters who pointed rifles through holes in the block-

Officers' quarters at Fort Davis in Texas. This was one of the U.S. Army's many Western forts without encircling walls.

house walls. Wooden blockhouses were often built into the corners of typical walled forts. Fort Dearborn, which once guarded the tiny settlement of Chicago, was one such fort.

Many of the last Western "forts" were not surrounded by walls either. These Army posts were clusters of buildings arranged around a parade ground where soldiers could practice marching and riding. The number of fighting Native Americans had been reduced so much that the Army had no fear of its forts being attacked.

IV INSIDE A FORT

*Protective earth mounds and moat at Fort Pulaski in Georgia.
The moat is sometimes used by alligators when their natural ponds
lack water.*

A British garrison that left the protection of Fort Michilimackinac, Michigan, in 1763 was destroyed by Pontiac and his Ottawa warriors.

Many forts' outer walls were surrounded by a ditch, or **moat**. Depending upon the fort, the ditch could be dry or filled with water. Water in the Fort Pulaski moat was 7 feet deep.

Inside the walls of a fort was the soldier's village — buildings that took care of his needs while he was stationed at the fort. The **barracks** was the building where most of the soldiers slept. Officers slept in separate, more comfortable rooms. Other structures typically found within a fort's walls were a chapel, ice house, stable, storehouse, powder magazine, cistern for water storage, and flagstaff. Moated forts had drawbridges that could be dropped across the moat for passage into or out of the fort.

Fort Sumter, South Carolina, was the scene of a Civil War battle between Confederate defenders and Union artillery.

Soldiers were often too warm, too cold or too crowded. Pay was low and military discipline was often tough. Boredom was a frequent complaint of soldiers because most forts in North America were never attacked. The forts were often used as prisons, military headquarters, and places where armies came to organize, rest and regroup. Forts that were attacked were sometimes the scenes of dreadful killing on both sides of the battle. A powder magazine at Fort Erie exploded during the War of 1812. About 1,000 British soldiers who were attacking the American-held fort were killed or injured. Perhaps Colonel Olmstead recalled that event when he surrendered Fort Pulaski.

Another fort horror story — just one of many during the Civil War — involved a young Union officer, Captain Robert Gould Shaw. Captain Shaw was the white officer in charge of a group of black soldiers from Massachusetts. The Union Army had just begun to enlist black soldiers. Captain Shaw was ordered to attack Fort Wagner near Charleston, South Carolina. The Union commanders thought artillery fire had weakened the fort. Believing this, he and his men approached the fort. They were wrong. Attacking the Confederate fort on foot, Captain Shaw led his men to glory — and slaughter.

Soldiers in a fort were sometimes trapped by an attacking force. Attackers showered forts with gunfire for hours, days or even months. Long-term attempts at

Big guns at Fort Ticonderoga, New York, boomed during the Revolutionary War.

capturing forts were called **sieges**. Some were successful; others failed. Fort Sumter in South Carolina was under siege by Union guns for 22 months during the Civil War. Her defenders finally abandoned the fort and slipped away during the night — but only after they had destroyed the fort's guns, so that the Union could not use them.

In 1860 people from the Navajo tribe in the Southwest surrounded and attacked Fort Defiance in New Mexico. Native American weapons were no match for Army defenses. Because of this, Native American attacks against American forts were extremely rare. Sioux warriors kept soldiers trapped in Fort Abercrombie, North Dakota, for six weeks in 1862. The Sioux couldn't

The Sioux kept Fort Abercrombie in North Dakota under siege for six weeks in 1862.

The massive Castillo de San Marcos in Florida was built by the Spanish in the 1600s. It flew the flags of four nations.

take the fort, but neither could the fort defenders leave. The Sioux eventually retreated.

Many forts changed hands through the centuries. Treaties between nations shifted ownership of land and forts. Actual battles also led to ownership changes. No fort, however, changed hands more often than a fort in St. Augustine, Florida. Built by the Spanish in the late 1600s, the rugged stone fort was christened Castillo de San Marcos. British forces twice attacked the fort during the 1700s, but without great success. However, in a land swap involving Britain, Spain and France, Florida and the fort were taken over by Britain in 1763. Spain regained Florida and the castillo in 1783. A few years later, Spain gave Florida to the United States. The castillo became Fort Marion. The Southern Confederacy took brief possession of the fort during the Civil War.

VI NORTH AMERICAN FORTS: A TOUR

The Great Rendezvous days are relived each summer at Fort William in Ontario.

There are many forts that you can visit in North America. Some of them have exciting and tragic histories of blood and thunder. Yet each fort, whether its days were violent or calm, is an interesting and important link with America's past. You can relive a sliver of the past by visiting a fort and learning more about its history. The United States National Park Service cares for about 25 forts and sites of old forts. Various organizations in Canada and the United States keep many other forts open for visitors, too. Costumed actors — **interpreters** — in some of the forts help show visitors what life was like there. Here is a brief look at just a few of the forts you can visit.

Ontario is a treasure chest of forts. Among the forts there are Erie, George, Henry and William. Fort Henry was built to defend Canada against the possibility of attack from the United States. That sounds foolish now, but when fort construction began in 1832, the Canadians were worried. By 1848, when the huge, costly stone fort was finished, relations between Canada and the U.S. were generally pleasant. Fort William is the site of a Great Rendezvous **re-enactment** each summer. People in 1820s costume act out the times of the Rendezvous. In Nova Scotia, the Fortress of Louisbourg National Historic Park is a restored French city-fort of the mid-1700s.

In Florida, the restored Castillo de San Marcos is a major attraction. Forts Sumter and Moultrie in South

For 18 years, Fort Larned, Kansas, was one of the major Army posts along the old Santa Fe Trail.

Carolina were scenes of heavy Civil War fighting. In Baltimore, Maryland, Fort McHenry National Monument and Historic Shrine is the site where the *Star Spangled Banner,* America's national anthem, was written. Francis Scott Key composed the song during a British attack on the fort during the War of 1812.

Several forts stand near the Great Lakes, including restored Forts Mackinac and Michilimackinac in Michigan. Built by the French in 1715, Michilimackinac was taken by the British army in 1761. Niagra, in New York, is another French-built fort that was taken by British soldiers during the French and Indian War (1754-63). Fort Ticonderoga, also in New York, was captured and later lost by the Americans during the Revolutionary War (1775-83) against Britain. Ticonderoga has been rebuilt, as has Fort Stanwix, another New York fort with roots in the American Revolution.

Fort Davis is one of the most impressive forts remaining in the American West. Built in 1854, it guarded the El Paso-San Antonio Road in West Texas. Wyoming's Fort Laramie, now restored, was busy from 1849-1890. Fort Larned, Kansas, was occupied between 1860-1878. It was a link in the chain of forts protecting the Santa Fe Trail between Missouri and New Mexico. The ghostly remains of Fort Bowie linger in the old Apache country of southern Arizona.

You can relax when you visit the old fortresses of North America. Though the stout walls no longer quake with explosions, and the old guns no longer fire in anger, they truly echo with the past.

GLOSSARY

artillery (are TIL er ee) - large, mounted firearms (guns) that are loaded and fired by a crew of soldiers

barracks (BARE ehks) - a building where soldiers are housed

blockhouse (BLAHK house) - a building of heavy timbers, or logs, built to withstand attack

colonist (KAHL un ihst) - a person who settles in a country other than the one in which he was born, such as a colonist from France settling in Canada

garrison (GAIR ih sun) - the soldiers who are stationed in a fort

interpreter (in TER pret er) - one who acts out or explains an event

magazine (MAG uh zeen) - a storage place or building for gunpowder

masonry (MAY sun ree) - stone or brickwork built in layers by a mason, or bricklayer

moat (MOTE) - a ditch, often filled with water, that encircles a fort or castle

palisade (PAL uh sade) - a fence of sharpened stakes built to keep enemies out

re-enactment (ree en AKT ment) - the re-creation of a historical event in order to educate or entertain

reservation (rez er VAY shun) - land set aside by a government for use by a particular group, such as Native Americans

restored (re STORD) - renewed, returned to the original condition

siege (SEEJ) - a long attack on a strongly defended position, such as a fort

strategic (struh TEE jihk) - of value for military purposes

INDEX